The "Art" of Getting Dumped

Written and Illustrated by:
Jonas

Published by:
Moonshadow & Max Publications
(A Division of J. & A. Industries, Inc.)
Chicago, Illinois USA
Tel: (773) 778-6649
Fax: (773) 778- 9678

Graphic Design by:
Blaise Graphics, Inc.
Chicago, Illinois USA
Tel: (773) 445-0979
Fax: (773) 445-0179

Printing and Color Separations by:
InterScan Graphics & Sanon Printing Corp S/B
Subang Jaya, Selangor, Malaysia
Tel: 03-732-0146
Fax: 03-732-0133

International Standard Book Number 0-9662-6440-1
Library of Congress Catalog Number 98-091188

First Edition, 1998

Printed in Malaysia

The Art of

Getting Dumped
by Jonas

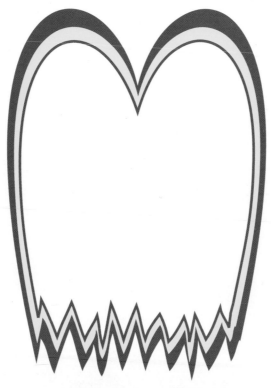

*Dedicated to everyone who
has ever had a broken heart.*

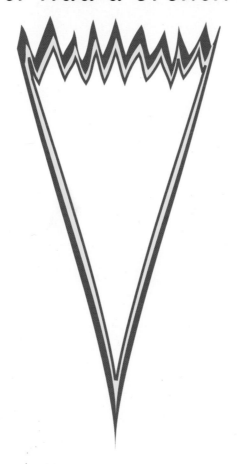

The heck with the optimism!
Forget the good cheer!
You've just been dumped
by the one you held dear!

Your life's been cruelly,
callously crushed...

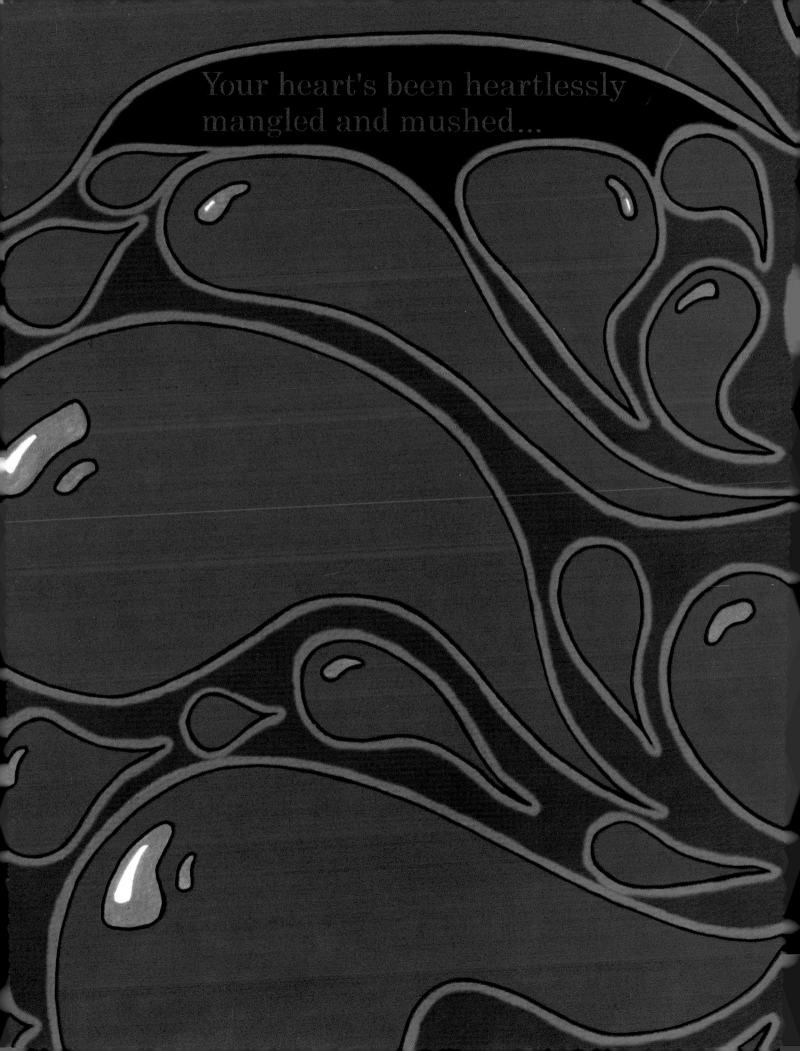

Your heart's been heartlessly
mangled and mushed...

Your head
is spinning.
Your stomach
says, "Vomit!"
You wish
you could.
You think
that might
calm it.

But, as you
most surely
now know,
there's
little to
help *this*
nausea go.

You can do nothing
but curl up and cry...

...so with that nothing to lose
you think, "One last try."

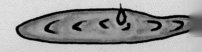

Clutching your stomach
you voice a small moan,
fleeing from fetal form,
feeling for the phone.

You hang up the phone,
clichés ringing in your head.
You grab the tissue box.
You crawl into bed.

Sleep! That's the ticket!
Oh, sweet relief!
Sleep is nature's best cure
for combatting grief.

And sleep is something
of which you do quite a lot,
sometimes finding it easy,
sometimes finding it not.

Lying in laundry, you close
your eyes and you dream,
vindictively, of course,
of your death unforeseen.

From a flaming wreck
racing to rescue a mutt,
you run in slow motion
until an explosion...

...buries a bumper deep in your butt.

Your beloved hearing
of your selfless act,
is now crying and sobbing
and wanting you back.

There's only one hitch
in this elaborate scheme...
in this fabulous plan...
in this grandiose dream.

It's back to the anguish, the nausea and pain. You've woken up and it's all the same.

All you're left with are questions unanswered by talking, so with no other option you resort to...

Whether you see what you wanted or something you shouldn't or something that you had hoped you wouldn't...

...solving your problem this pursuit just couldn't.

Cookies!

Ice cream!

Chocolate cake!

Cheeseburgers!
French fries!
Junk food galore!
Donuts! Ding Dongs!
You only want more!

Food! How wonderful!
Food helps you endure.
But, soon you discover
that food's not the cure.

So taking things to the other extreme, you exercise constantly to make your body lean.

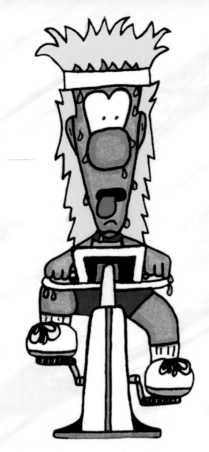

"I refuse to be fat... to waddle and toddle. I'll show them. I'll look like a model!"

As you work out to be more agile and nimble, your new goal now... to be a sex symbol.

But, even though
exercise is great,
it's not the outside that
carries the weight.

Your heart's what's heavy.
Life seems horribly unfair.
However, you find it hurts less
when you choose not to care.

And now each new day
gets a little easier to face,
because each time the phone
rings your heart doesn't race.

Now even though this
apathy brings some relief,
your indulgence in this
is best if it's brief.

What you feel next you might
not believe that it's true.
You wish your "ex" happiness
even without you.

First, you may listen to sad love songs at home
finally feeling their meaning...feeling less alone.
Or, you become a recluse and assume your fate
is to watch bad sitcoms...T.V. as your mate.

You're quite cozy and content, but interfering friends that are couples, decide to step in...

...and convince you to double.

You may begin
to believe that
there is no
one for you,
but then one
surprising day say,
"I don't have
to be blue.
I don't have
to be sad.
I don't need
someone to meet.
I don't need
someone else
to make *myself*
complete!"

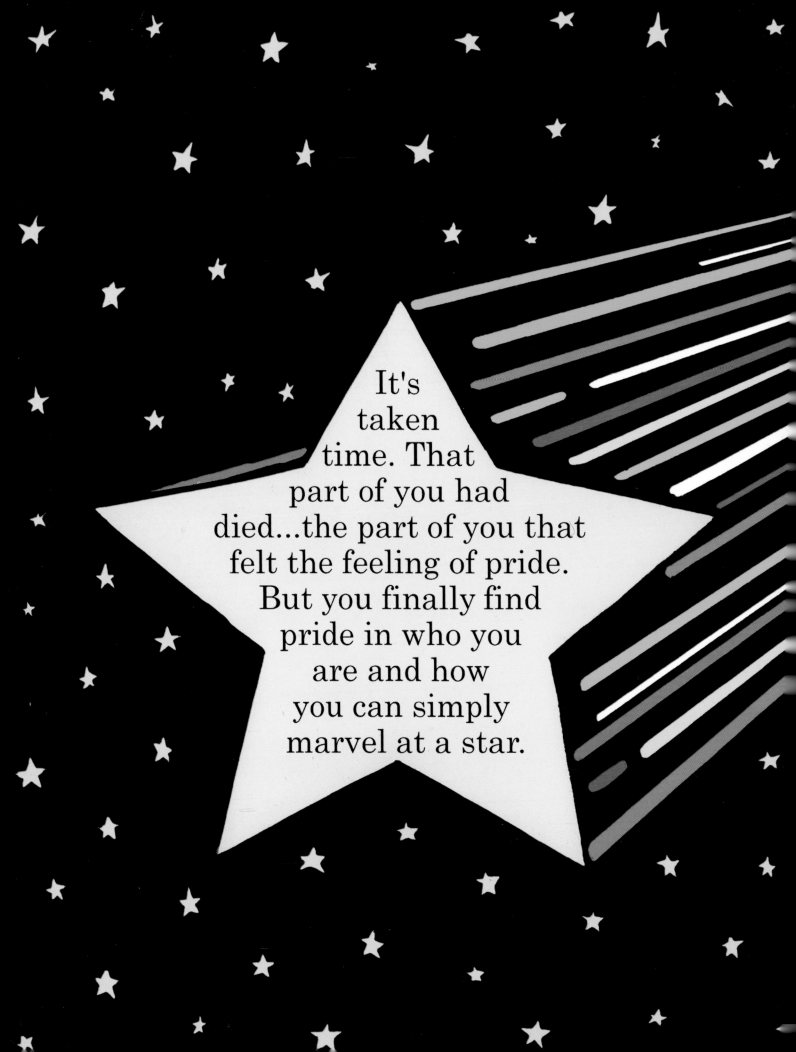

It's taken time. That part of you had died...the part of you that felt the feeling of pride. But you finally find pride in who you are and how you can simply marvel at a star.

Now your world is more cheery. Your outlook... more bright. You're feeling better about yourself and everything in sight.

And so the old adage is
quite possibly true.
Time heals all wounds...
even those inflicted on you.

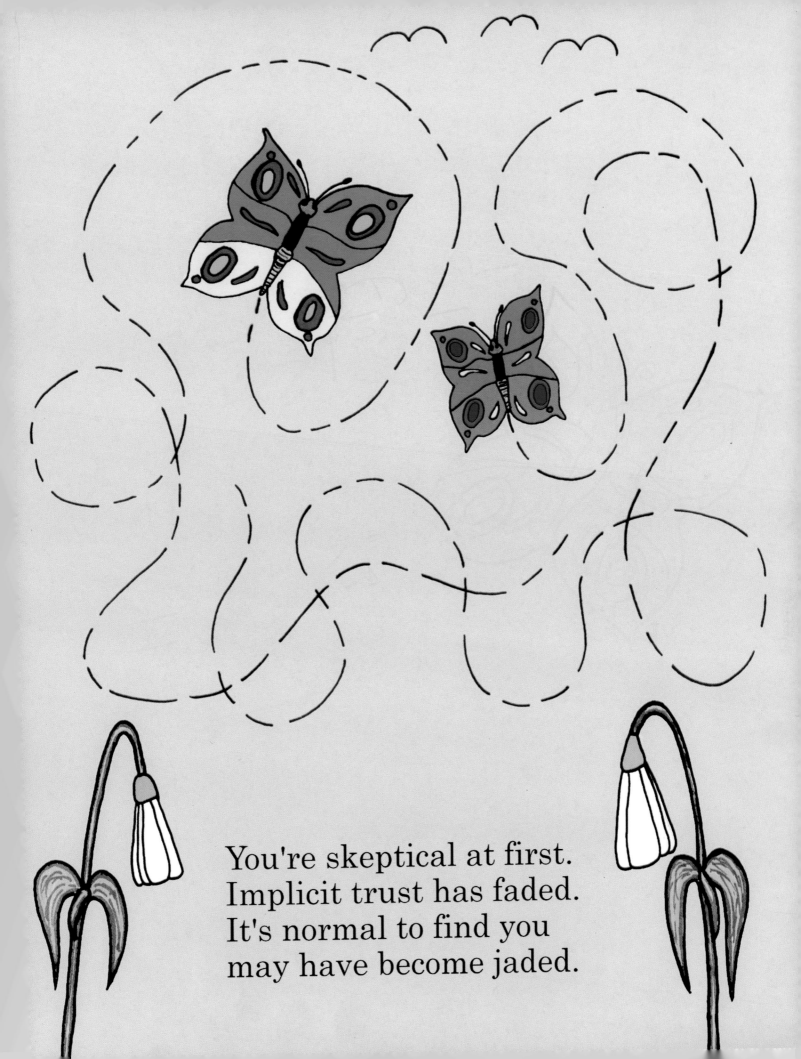

You're skeptical at first.
Implicit trust has faded.
It's normal to find you
may have become jaded.

Around the next corner, the sun may be shining and the sky may be blue, and opportunity may be waiting... and it may be waiting for *you*.

And it may hurt to recall
the tears that you cried,
but in the end it's simply
worse not having tried.

Just trust in Life!
You most surely should!
Make it your motto...

"Life...is good."

Acknowledgements

I have endless gratitude for...

my mother, from whose example I learn to appreciate the beauty of a flower and receive strength and joy from nature's amazing treasures.

my father, who taught me the importance of getting up no matter how many times you're knocked down.

my brother, Paul, who let me get behind in the rent while working on this book, or in other words, for being a brother.

Lana, who told me of the importance of pursuing one's dreams from the beginning which ironically lead to my first broken heart which lead to this book.

Chuck, Dan, John, Lisa, and all my other friends, whose convictions and faith in this book never faltered even when mine sometimes did.

Alex, of Blaise Graphics, Inc., whose computer wizardry and patience made this book possible, and who became more than just someone I paid large sums of money to, but a friend as well.

Moonshadow, who graciously shared some of her nine lives with me, and *Max,* whose sweet innocence and wonderment of the world I aspire to attain.

the women who have broken my heart, as well as those who haven't, for contributing to different chapters in my life, this book, and to my personal growth.

finally, and most importantly...***Life.***